Woodstock was not about sex, drugs, and rock and roll.
It was about spirituality, about love, about sharing,
about helping each other, living in peace and harmony.
— Richie Havens

WOODSTOCK
MUSIC & ART FAIR

presents

AN
AQUARIAN
EXPOSITION
in
WHITE LAKE, N.Y.*

3 DAYS of PEACE & MUSIC

AUGUST
15, 16, 17.

One day $7.00. Two days $13.00. Three days $16.00.

For tickets and information write to:
WOODSTOCK MUSIC
BOX 996, RADIO CITY STATION
NEW YORK 10019

Skolnick

*White Lake, Town of Bethel, Sullivan County, N.Y.

WITH

FRI., AUG. 15
Joan Baez
Arlo Guthrie
Tim Hardin
Richie Havens
Incredible String Band
Ravi Shankar
Sly And The Family Stone
Bert Sommer
Sweetwater

SAT., AUG. 16
Canned Heat
Creedence Clearwater
Grateful Dead
Keef Hartley
Janis Joplin
Jefferson Airplane
Mountain
Quill
Santana
The Who

SUN., AUG. 17
The Band
Jeff Beck Group
Blood, Sweat and Tears
Joe Cocker
Crosby, Stills and Nash
Jimi Hendrix
Iron Butterfly
Ten Years After
Johnny Winter

ART SHOW
Paintings and sculptures on trees, on grass, surrounded by the Hudson valley, will be displayed. Works by artists, ghetto artists, and accomplished artists will be glad to discuss their work, or the un-special calendar of the surroundings, or anything else that might be on your mind. If you're an artist, and you want to display, write for information.

CRAFTS BAZAAR
If you like creative knickknacks and old junk you'll love roaming around our bazaar. You'll see imaginative leather, ceramic, bead, and silver creations, as well as Zodiac Charts, camp clothes, and worn out shoes.

If you like playing with beads, or improvising on a guitar, or writing poetry, or molding clay, step by one of our work shops and see what you can give and take.

FOOD
There will be cakes and hotdogs and dozens of curious food and fruit combinations to experiment with.

HUNDREDS OF ACRES
TO ROAM ON
Walk around for three days without seeing a skyscraper or a traffic light. Fly a kite, sun yourself. Cook your own food and breathe unspoiled air. Camp out; water and restrooms will be supplied. Tents and camping equipment will be available at the Camp Store.

MUSIC STARTS AT 4:00 P.M. ON FRIDAY, AND AT 1:00 P.M. ON SATURDAY AND SUNDAY.

It'll run for 12 continuous hours, except for a few short breaks to allow the performers to catch their breath.

woodstock

1969

the first festival

3 DAYS OF PEACE & MUSIC

A PHOTO COMMEMORATIVE

PRODUCED BY ELLIOTT LANDY

SQUAREBOOKS

DEDICATED TO THE FUTURE

We are interested in seeing your Woodstock '69 stories, photographs, and films
for future projects. If you were there and want to share your experience with us,
or if you want to receive a list of Woodstock-related items for sale,
or information about museum-quality photographic prints,
please write to LandyVision, POB 836, Woodstock, NY 12498.

SQUAREBOOKS
PO BOX 6699
SANTA ROSA, CA 95406

1 2 3 4 5 6 7 8 9 0

ISBN: 0-916290-74-3 (SOFTBOUND)
ISBN: 0-916290-75-1 (HARDBOUND)

Creative Director: Elliott Landy
Art Direction and Design: Eric Schmidt
Text Editor: Diana Oestreich-Landy
Produced by LandyVision
Copy Editor: Daia Gerson
Computer: Adam Zaretsky

A joint venture of
LANDYVISION & SQUAREBOOKS

Printed in Italy

THE THING ABOUT WOODSTOCK WAS THAT YOU COULD FEEL THE PRESENCE OF
INVISIBLE TIME TRAVELERS FROM THE FUTURE WHO HAD COME BACK TO SEE IT.
YOU COULD SENSE THE SIGNIFICANCE OF THE EVENT AS IT WAS HAPPENING.
THERE WAS A KIND OF SWOLLEN HISTORICITY—A TRULY PREGNANT MOMENT.
YOU DEFINITELY KNEW THAT THIS WAS A MILESTONE, IT WAS IN THE AIR.

AS A HUMAN BEING I HAD A WONDERFUL TIME, HANGING OUT WITH FRIENDS
IN THE MUSIC BUSINESS AND SHARING GREAT LITTLE JAMS. BUT OUR PERFOR-
MANCE ONSTAGE—THE DEAD'S PART IN WOODSTOCK—WAS MUSICALLY A TOTAL
DISASTER THAT IS BEST LEFT FORGOTTEN. I'VE CERTAINLY BEEN TRYING TO FOR-
GET IT FOR 25 YEARS.

YET OTHER MUSICIANS HAD THEIR CAREERS EXPLODE THERE. IT WAS TRULY
A SPECIAL MOMENT, WHICH YOU CAN STILL HEAR AND SEE.

AS FAR AS THE PHOTOGRAPHERS GO, I KNOW ALL THESE RASCALS. I'VE
STOOD IN FRONT OF THEIR CAMERAS AND HAVE HAD THEIR ANTICS AS SIDEBAR
EXPERIENCES FOR MY ENTIRE CAREER. BUT I'VE ALWAYS ENJOYED THEIR WORK.
NOW YOU CAN TOO.
JERRY GARCIA.

Bethel Pilgrims Smoke 'Grass' And Some Take LSD to 'Groove'

Special to The New York Times

BETHEL, N. Y., Aug. 17—A billowy haze of sweet smoke rose through purple spotlights from the sloping hillside where throngs of young people—their average age about 20—sat or sprawled in the midnight darkness and listened to the rock music.

The smoke was not from campfires.

"There was so much grass being smoked last night that you could get stoned just sitting there breathing," said a 19-year-old student from Denison University in Ohio. "It got so you didn't even want another drag of anything."

In the argot of the drug scene — and the Woodstock Music and Art Fair was the focus of that scene in the northeast this weekend — "grass" is marijuana, and getting "stoned" is getting high on it.

"How many of the crowd are smoking grass?" scores of youths were asked in a spot check of the situation.

The almost unanimous response was: Ninety-nine per cent.

Many people who are not, as the young people say, "into the drug scene," find it incredible that marijuana can be so prevalent and so widely used despite the fact that its sale or possession is illegal.

By the tens of thousands, youths smoked marijuana in "joints"—which are hand-rolled cigarettes with marijuana inside — in water pipes, brass pipes, hookahs and ornate Indian pipes.

They smoked quite openly, not fearing to be "busted," at least not within the confines of the 600-acre farm where the action is.

State troopers said, however, that they had made a least 80 arrests here on narcotics charges, including about a dozen on the festival grounds on a charge of selling.

In explaining the few arrests on the fairgrounds, one policeman said there were not enough jails in the county to hold those breaking the law.

"Grass" was not the only thing used here. There was also—unfortunately for scores of youngsters, and deadly for at least one so far—LSD, popularly called acid because of its chemical name, lysergic acid diethylamide; amphetamines like dexadrine, popularly called "speed"; and assorted other drugs that are "dropped" or "popped" or "toked" or sniffed or swallowed.

To most people not acquainted with the drug scene—which includes most of those on the far side of the "generation gap"—what went on here was simply incomprehensible at best, and a flagrant violation of law and morals at worst.

But there were few people in the throng here who agreed. Nonetheless, there was worry and sometimes scorn for the "freaks" who put almost any chemical into their mouths, lungs or veins.

'Grooving' on the Sounds

A number of the youths here said that the so-called "soft drugs," like marijuana, some milder forms of hashish and, on the strongest side, mescalin, were used primarily because they produce a euphoria and, in the setting of rock music, allow the users to "groove" on the sounds.

This means that the electronically amplified vibrations are heard almost to the exclusion of any other extraneous sounds. It is a kind of intense concentration, according to many of the marijuana users who came to the festival.

When the "stoned" listeners "groove" on the music what happens, as one 22-year-old mathematics major from Boston College put it, is this:

"You can hear every sound, every click of the guitar pick. When you get a really heavy group [a heavy group, roughly translated, means one that uses hard driving bass notes and complex percussion rhythms] you can feel the music actually hitting you. Most of the rock music nowadays is played by stoned people for stoned people."

By BARNARD L. COLLIER
Special to The New York Times

BETHEL, N. Y., Monday, Aug. 18 — Waves of weary youngsters streamed away from the Woodstock Music and Art Fair last night and early today as security officials reported at least two deaths and 4,000 people treated for injuries, illness and adverse drug reactions over the festival's three-day period.

However, festival officials said the folk and rock music could go on until dawn, and most of the crowd was determined to stay on.

Campfires Burn

As the music wailed on into the early morning hours, more than 100 campfires — fed by fence-posts and any other wood the young people could lay their hands on—flickered around the hillside that formed a natural amphitheater for the festival.

By midnight nearly half of the 300,000 fans who had camped here for the weekend had left. A thunderstorm late yesterday afternoon provided the first big impetus to depart, and a steady stream continued to leave through the night.

Drugs and auto traffic continued to be the main headaches.

But the crowd itself was extremely well-behaved. As Dr. William Abruzzi, the festival's chief medical officer, put it: "There has been no violence whatsoever, which is remarkable for a crowd of this size. These people are really beautiful."

Months of Planning

Local merchants and residents eased the food shortage. Youths who endured drenching rain to hear such pop performers as Sly and the Family Stone and the Creedence Clearwater Revival overcame the water shortage by gulping down soft drinks and beer. And as the close of the festival approached, the spirits of the audience —mostly youths of 17 to 20— were high.

For many, the weekend had been the fulfillment of months of planning and hoping, not only to see and hear the biggest group of pop performers ever assembled, but also to capture the excitement of camping out with strangers, experimenting with drugs and sharing — as one youth put it —"an incredible unification."

The state police said last night that traffic was moving out of the area at a gradual and slow but steady pace. Throughout the weekend, parked and stalled cars had been stretched out on the roads in all directions.

The state police said they had about 150 men on duty to help deal with the traffic in a 20-mile radius. They were permitting no cars to enter the area.

Drugs Kill a Youth

Helicopters ferried out some youths who had fallen ill. About 100 people were treated yesterday for bad reactions to drugs, bringing to 400 the number of persons so treated during the three-day affair.

The pervasive use of drugs at the festival resulted in one death yesterday. The unidentified youth was taken to Horton Memorial Hospital in Middletown, N. Y., where officials said he failed to respond to treatment for what was believed to be an overdose of heroin.

Three young men were taken to the Middletown hospital yesterday in critical condition as a result of drug overdoses. One of them, identified as George Xikis, 18 years old, of Astoria, Queens, also suffered a fractured skull when he fell from a car roof while under the influence of drugs, hospital officials said.

The two others in critical condition were identified as Anthony Gencarelli, 18, of Port Chester, N. Y., and Arkie Melunow, 22, of Franklin Township, N. J.

Despite the "bad trips" of many drug users at the festival, sales were made openly. Festival officials made periodic announcements from the stage that impure and harmful drugs were circulating in the crowd.

The use of heroin and LSD, popularly known as "acid" because of its chemical name, lysergic acid diethylamide, drew the public warnings. But marijuana was the most widely used drug, with many youths maintaining that practically everyone in the audience was smoking.

Only about 80 arrests were made on drug charges, a dozen inside the fair grounds. In addition to the death attributed to the overdose, one other youth was reported killed. The police identified him as Raymond R. Mizsak, 17, of Trenton, and said he had been run over by a tractor yesterday morning.

2 Babies Born

Dr. Abruzzi said yesterday that first-aid facilities were returning to normal after the arrival of medical supplies and a dozen doctors summoned as volunteers.

Dr. Abruzzi said two babies were born during the course of the festival, one in a car caught in traffic on nearby Route 17B and the other in a hospital after a helicopter flight from the festival site. He said four miscarriages also were reported.

Though the festival was to end early today, there was no assurance that the crowds would vanish quickly. Anticipating massive traffic tie-ups in the area, many in the crowd said they would remain encamped for a day or two on the 600-acre farm of Max Yasgur that was rented for the event.

"Some of them might decide to live here permanently," one state trooper said.

Many of the fans, weary after listening to entertainment that started Saturday night and continued until 8 A.M. yesterday, slept late yesterday morning and into the afternoon. Most slept in the open and others in the thousands of tents surrounding the entertainment area.

Later, brightened their outlook and began to dry the mud left by Friday night's heavy rains.

"The whole thing is a gas,"

said one long-haired young man, who identified himself as "Speed." "I dig it all," he said, "the mud, the rain, the music, the hassles."

When the rains came yesterday, however, the crowd began to break.

The storm, which struck at 4:30 P.M. after a sunny and breezy day, would have washed out any less-determined crowds. But at least 80,000 young people sat or stood in front of the stage and shouted obscenities at the darkened skies as trash rolled down the muddy hillside with the runoff of the rain. Others took shelter in dripping tents, lean-tos, cars and trucks.

The festival promoters decided to continue the show but

also to try to persuade as much of the audience as possible to leave the area for their cars or some sort of shelter.

The problem was, however, that most of those who remained unsheltered had parked their cars many miles from the festival grounds.

"It is really a problem because the kids are as wet as they can get already and they have miles to go before they can even hope to get dry," said Michael Lang, the executive producer of the festival.

The threat of bronchial disease and influenza was increased by the downpour, according to staff doctors here. Many boys and girls wandered through the storm nude, red mud clinging to their bodies.

When the storm stuck, the performer on the stage, Joe Cocker, stopped playing and the hundreds of people on the plywood and steel structure scurried off for fear of its being toppled by the winds, which were blowing in gusts estimated at up to 40 miles an hour.

Amplifiers and other electronic devices were covered to avoid damage, and recorded music was played for the crowd.

Naked Man Cheered

As performers wandered onto the stage to look at the crowd and to decide whether to play, they were greeted by loud cheering. One naked man also came up on stage and danced.

At 6:15 P.M. the sun broke through and spirits rose again.

Artie Cornfield, a partner in the festival production company, said, "I guess this was meant to happen, and everybody is still with us. We're going to go on all night with the music."

Some Fans Reach Here

Young people straggling into the Port of New York Authority bus terminal at 41st Street and Eighth Avenue last night were damp, disheveled and given to such wild eccentricities of dress as the wearing of a battered top hat with a grimy jersey, blue jeans and sandals.

They were, according to a driver, Richard Biccum, "good kids in disguise." Mr. Biccum, who is 26 years old, said: "I'll haul kids any day rather than commuters," because they were exceptionally polite and orderly.

Reginald Dorsey, a Short Line Bus System dispatcher, agreed that the youths were "beautiful people" who had caused no trouble.

Farmer With Soul

Max Yasgur

Special to The New York Times

BETHEL, N. Y., Aug. 17— Until a few days ago Max Yasgur was just another dairy farmer in Sullivan County. Now he gets phone calls threatening to burn him out. And even more calls praising him and asking how the callers can help. The reason for his unwonted prominence is

Man in the News

that it was on 600 acres of his land that hundreds of thousands of youngsters gathered for Woodstock Music and Art Fair, their cars blocking roads and overflowing onto lawns.

But Mr. Yasgur, a dairy farmer since boyhood, has the stubbornness of most farmers. He also avoids the phone these days.

"I never expected this festival to be this big," he told an acquaintance the other day. "But if the generation gap is to be closed, we older people have to do more than we have done."

He Gives Away Food

A gaunt man of 49, with glasses, he looks even taller than his 5 feet 11 inches. He is trying to do his bit to bridge the generation gap by giving large amounts of dairy products to the youngsters at the festival, sometimes at cost and often free.

His red barn, fronting on Route 17B, with its long line of parked cars, displays a big sign reading, "Free Water."

He put up this sign when he heard that some residents were selling water to the youngsters at the festival. He slammed a work-hardened fist down on the table and demanded of some friends:

"How can anyone ask for money for water?"

The other day, as he was preparing to give away substantial quantities of butter and cheese, someone asked what the youngsters would put the butter on.

That evening a relative brought a car filled with loaves of bread to the farm.

Mr. Yasgur and his wife, Miriam, have two children, a daughter, Lois, and a son, Samuel, who is an assistant district attorney on the staff of District Attorney Frank S. Hogan of Manhattan.

The gently rolling Yasgur farm is the home of a herd of 650 cows, mostly Guernsey. Mr. Yasgur raises some of the corn used as feed for his dairy herd.

Friends Concerned on Health

As he paces nervously in the heavy work shoes he has worn almost all his life, his friends become increasingly concerned. He has a cardiac history and they fear another heart attack.

Mr. Yasgur has been getting very little sleep at night and refuses to ease up during the day, often flying over the music festival area in a helicopter.

A man in this county who has known Mr. Yasgur for many years, and who thinks the festival was a terrible mistake, said:

"I don't doubt that Max made a good business deal. But I think he was motivated at least as much by his principles as by the thought of making money." Sponsors of the fair said they had paid $50,000 to rent the farm.

And a successful businessman who has been dealing with the dairy farmer for a long time declared:

"Max is not just a successful farmer. He is an individualist."

By MIKE JAHN
Special to The New York Times

BETHEL, N. Y., Monday, Aug. 18—The Band, the country-rock group that once was Bob Dylan's backup band, left the stage just before midnight last night as the Woodstock Music and Art Fair braced for another dusk-to-dawn session.

The group plays a taut fusion of country music and rock with vocals direct from the classic nasal hillbilly style.

It followed a raucus display of California "psychedelic" rock by Country Joe and the Fish and a low-key concert of blues rock by Ten Years After, a British band.

•

Mainly because of the weather, the performers arrived on stage about eight hours behind schedule, playing to a greatly reduced audience, most of it a hard-core group of rock 'n' roll devotees.

Yesterday's program began with Sly and The Family Stone, the innovative rock band from San Francisco, which completely captured the audience's imagination.

The group appeared early in the morning, and by the end of its hour-and-a-half stint had almost everybody within earshot dancing or clapping. Spotlights made great swoops across the crowd and people threw sparklers into the air every time the group shouted "Higher!" as part of one of their songs.

When Sly and the Family Stone went onstage at about 3 A.M., the audience had been sitting or lying for a long time and was ripe for some exercise.

The group, which is led by a former San Francisco disk jockey, Sylvester ("Sly") Stone, has artfully risen above the mass of soul bands by using melody styles vastly different from what is usual in soul music.

The best example of the group's sound fusion is "Everyday People," its song about brotherhood, which became one of the most popular records released this year. Sly and the Family Stone has managed to combine a happy-sounding melody line with an infectious and very danceable soul beat

The crowd here responded many times more warmly than to any of the groups or individuals that appeared earlier.

One of those groups was Creedence Clearwater Revival, a band from San Francisco. It gave a good concert of its blues-rock and traditional rock songs. Led by the gritty voice and spunky guitar of the group's leader, John Fogerty, the group played beautiful versions of its familiar songs, "Proud Mary," "Born on the Bayou" and "I Put a Spell on You."

Unlike many other West Coast groups, Creedence Clearwater Revival plays simple, unsophisticated and rollicking music. The group formed in 1959 when the members were in junior high school and has been together ever since. This is no small achievement considering that most rock groups fall apart after about a year.

Janis Joplin, the Texas singer, who became so popular as a member of the now disbanded San Francisco group Big Brother and The Holding Company, sang on Saturday night with her own band, as yet unnamed.

The special meaning of this concert for Miss Joplin is that her career was given its biggest push by the 1967 Monterey Pop Festival in California, the first of these large rock gatherings.

Her appearance here was less spectacular. She sang hard and loud and was well received but there were problems. Miss Joplin is a very emotional singer given to great outbursts of energy. Big Brother and The Holding Company was similarly inclined. Precision was dropped in favor of spontaneity and excitement, and it was a happy bargain. Her new band is 10 times more precise and technically correct than Big Brother, but much less exciting.

•

Miss Joplin sang some of her well-known songs, like "Piece of My Heart" and the Bee Gees's "To Love Somebody." One of her best new songs, "Work Me, Lord," was written by Nick Gravenites, singer for another defunct band, The Electric Flag.

Saturday also saw performances by Canned Heat, The Grateful Dead and The Who. Jefferson Airplane, the San Francisco band, played a long set that ushered in the dawn.

BY JOHN MORRIS

TWENTY-FIVE YEARS AGO, IN THE AGE OF ACCIDENTS, IN THE TIME OF FREE-FLOWING THOUGHT, UNBRIDLED ENERGY, AND EXPANDING LOVE, A CURLY-HEADED KID PERSUADED A GROUP OF SUPPOSEDLY SANE PEOPLE THAT IT WOULD BE FUN TO PUT TOGETHER THIRTY BANDS, SIXTY HOG FARMERS, TWENTY-FIVE INDIANS, AND THREE HUNDRED WORKERS IN A FIELD IN UPSTATE NEW YORK AND HAVE A FESTIVAL AND INVITE THE WORLD— WHO CAME.

FOR THREE DAYS AND THREE NIGHTS CHRIS, MEL, STAN, LEE, JOEL, PENNY, JOHN, CHIP, WAVY, AND MANY, MANY OTHERS KEPT THE WATER RUNNING, THE FOOD ARRIVING, THE COMMUNICATIONS FUNCTIONING, THE MEDICAL TENTS SUPPLIED, AND THE MUSIC FLOWING.

FOR THREE DAYS AND THREE NIGHTS THE HUNDREDS OF THOUSANDS THAT FLOODED MAX'S FARM HILLS SHARED, LAUGHED, GOT WET, SHARED SOME MORE, LISTENED, NAPPED, ATE, TALKED, SANG, AND SHARED SOME MORE, AND WITH NOT ONE ACT OF PHYSICAL VIOLENCE SHOWED THE WORLD WHAT A GENERATION WAS MADE OF, WHAT PEACE, LOVE, AND MUSIC WERE REALLY ALL ABOUT.

IT WAS FUN, IT WAS MAGIC. IT WAS ALSO UNDERSTOOD THAT IT WAS IMPORTANT, IT WAS A RISK, IT WAS UNIQUE. IT WAS ENTERTAINMENT AT ITS BEST.

IT WAS RESPONSIBILITY WITH FLOWERS IN ITS HAIR. IT WAS THE GARDEN, IT WAS WOODSTOCK. IT WAS SOMETHING EVERY FACE IN THIS BOOK CARRIES IN HIS OR HER HEART AND IS PROUD OF.

JOHN MORRIS   I had run Filmore East for Bill Graham, so I knew most of the agents. The Who had turned us down. Frank Barcelone, who is the president of Premiere Talent, was and is one of the major rock-and-roll agents. He has U2 and Springstein, and in those days he had the Who and Steve Winwood.

We had Pete Townshend to dinner at Frank's apartment. We fed him, started pouring wine into him, and talked about Woodstock. Peter kept saying, "No, we don't want to." We kept pouring brandy into him on top of the wine, and about five o'clock in the morning Peter was sitting in the corner all scrunched up saying, "All right. I'll play the thing. Can I go to sleep? Please?"

David Bird, the hot poster designer of that period, did a very art-nouveau, beautiful, very elaborate poster. It was printed, but it just wasn't right. Arnie Skulnick, who did the poster in the end, had a four-year-old-daughter who was playing with construction materials and little blunt scissors, cutting things out. Arnie couldn't come up with an idea when suddenly he went, "Oh." He picked up her paper and scissors, cut out the bird and the arm of the guitar, walked in the next day, and said, "Here." We said, "Wow," and that was the poster. Total accident.

We had about four hundred people working at the site who had just shown up to help. Chris Langhart, our technical director would say, "Okay, who's a carpenter?" and whoever held up their hands, they were carpenters for a day. "Who's a plumber?" And when the guy who said he was a carpenter smashed his thumb or the plumber taped himself to the pipe, Langhart would shift him over to another crew, and that was how Langhart handled the labor. We never advertised for helpers. Al Aronowitz, a columnist for the *New York Post*, followed Langhart from making his early-morning cattle call, with "Who's a carpenter? Who's a plumber?" to digging holes, putting in wells, distributing pipes, getting telephone lines in, and he wrote this article that appeared on the first day of Woodstock. As I read it, the first thing I read was this typo, because he said, "I spent the day yesterday with the technical man, Chris Langhart," only the typo was Christ Langhart, and it was a miracle because the man finally got the credit he deserved. People don't write about the guys who build things and make it all happen.

The rain made it miserable. It wasn't even worth wearing raincoats or boots. It was warm and humid. It made the construction insane. People were working in mud up to their knees, building roads, putting in telephone lines. Everything was soaking wet, so everything got slowed to death.

The largest single concert anybody had had before Woodstock was the Beatles at Shea Stadium, which was fifty-five thousand people. Monterey, which had been a year or two before, was thirty-five thousand people over three days. The first words said at Woodstock publicly over the P.A. were me saying, "Holy shit," and about six hundred thousand people laughed. I can remember feeling a very heavy responsibility, realizing that what you say is going to have a very strong influence on the crowd getting along, having a good time, going through all the rainstorms, the heat, and cooperating with one another. And we had some very good people like Wavy saying, "We're going to make breakfast in bed for six hundred thousand people."

During the planning I went down to Santa Fe, New Mexico, to an Indian school and brought twenty-five American Indian kids to Woodstock. They came up with the Hog Farm on the plane. They were part of the arts fair, but they never got to show their art. Instead they ended up showing people how to build campfires.

The Hog Farm was brought in to set up a camping area. They became our security because the cops were pulled off by the police commissioner in New York, although a bunch of them did come up anyway. The Hog Farm was there to organize East Coast kids who were not used to camping. These kids showed up with penny loafers and a can of beans in a paper bag and forgot to bring a can opener. The Hog Farm ran a commune down in the Southwest and had organized major events.

Lisa Law, who was one of them, was the only woman that I've ever dealt with in my life who thoroughly terrorized me. She came into my office in my trailer and said, "Give me three thousand dollars to feed people. If you don't give it to me, they're going to starve." And this was three days before the festival. She does this whole number, I mean literally, putting me up against the wall, with "I gotta have this,

that"...and I thought three thousand dollars is cheap to get rid of this woman. I wrote a check and handed it to her, and she proceeded to go straight to New York to do exactly the same thing to John Roberts, get another three thousand dollars, and go buy five hundred pounds of bulgur wheat and three hundred pounds of rice. She probably fed a quarter of a million people during the festival who didn't have money to buy concession things. They just set up this gigantic kitchen that operated twenty-four hours a day throughout the whole festival, and she did exactly what she said she was going to do. Lisa is a friend to this day. She keeps saying to me, "How come you're not scared of me anymore?"

It became a free festival because everybody was already in before the fences were completed. All of a sudden the field was entirely full of people. There was a conference immediately. Artie Kornfeld suggested that we have collection baskets in the audience. I threw my hands in the air like, "Oh, now I've heard everything." I called John Roberts and Joel Rosenman in the White Lake office, and they agreed there was no way to move vast numbers of people out of that field. John was making a major decision, he was kissing a couple of million dollars good-bye. A pretty heavy decision for a twenty-six-year-old. He was an absolute gentleman at all times. After the festival he made sure that absolutely everybody got paid. I have a lot of respect for him.

We had planned this concert that we thought was going to draw seventy-five thousand people. In fact I had a bet with Michael Lang, which he has never asked me to pay, that I would give him one hundred dollars for every thousand people over seventy-five thousand. I never added up—and thank goodness Michael's never added up—how much I would have owed him, but suddenly there were six hundred thousand people in the field and another million and a half trying to get in. We're hiring helicopters, getting water, very different from a laid-back concert. We were suddenly in the city-management business dealing with serious risk to life and limb.

The governor of the state of New York had decided he was going to send in the National Guard and send all these people home. So I spent the first part of Friday arguing with Rockefeller's people. Thank

God I was able to prevent what would have become Attica.

One of the nicer things was when the state police said that during the festival there was not one case of physical violence. What almost broke that was this group called Tom Newman and the Crazies, from the Lower East Side. We got word that they were going to burn down the concession stands because "food should be free." Someone went on stage—myself or Abbie Hoffman, who was there with the yippies—and asked people to get around the concession stands and make sure that nobody caused any trouble. These guys came. They had bandannas over their heads. They were Maoists at that time—you know, they had read the book—and they came charging out and literally got smothered by about thirty to forty thousand people, who said, "Hey, man, cool it, I mean they're not great hot dogs, but they're the hot dogs we have." And, boom. It just calmed down with no physical violence whatsoever.

Richie Havens was the first act because we suddenly realized that we did not have any way to get artists from their hotels. The state police have a satellite photograph showing an immediate twenty-mile area, and seventeen miles in a circle around that site blocked solid. That's why we got the helicopters, because we figured it was the only way to get people in. I literally turned around to Annie, my then-wife, and said, "Look up 'Helicopter' in the Yellow Pages and hire every single one." I grabbed Richie and said, "I know you're not supposed to be on until third or whatever, but you're here." He played three encores, but he didn't know any more songs. I begged him to go out one more time, so he went out and started strumming and singing "Freedom" That's how the song was invented.

It was an accident that Swami Satchidinanda came saying that he would like to speak to the audience. And I thought "I haven't got any acts, so why not? Let's put him on with all his followers sitting around him." He talked about peace and leveled everything out. We surmounted thing after thing because there was such goodwill.

Friday was sort of peaceful and calm. Everybody curled up and covered themselves. Baez sang "Ave Maria" and some of her greats. Her wonderful voice put everybody to sleep. We got drizzle on Saturday—it was okay—can we have some sun, please? And on Sunday it was fabulous. Then we got a tornado. The winds were over fifty-five miles per hour. The great thing was Cocker was singing, and it made it feel like he had rustled it up. Twenty minutes before, I was trying to see if we could get fire trucks in to spray the crowd because it was so hot. All this moisture was coming up from the ground and we were starting to get heat-prostration problems, and then, thank you, we didn't need the fire engines.

We did ask Rockefeller's people for more medical facilities. We lost three people, I believe. One kid who put his sleeping bag down between a trailer and a tractor, and in the middle of the night he was accidentally run over. And two other guys died in hospitals. One was a Marine who had come out of Vietnam, had some kind of malarial disease, and was misdiagnosed as being a heroin overdose. The other had a burst appendix. Most of the medical problems were cut feet, heat, or sunburn exposure. I was on stage, and it looked like those opening scenes from *Apocalypse Now* where I see a formation of Hueys flying in, and I'm saying, "Uh-oh, when the audience sees this, they are going to be really upset, and we've got a problem." Then I saw the red crosses and said, "Ladies and gentlemen, the United States Army Medical Corps, come to help us." The roar of the crowd almost knocked the helicopters out of the air. It went from something that could have been really nasty to something that became totally positive. And they were a big help, they were great.

During the bad thunderstorm I almost had a nervous breakdown. The scaffolding towers, which weighed five hundred to six hundred pounds apiece, were swaying. Our immediate concern was to get people away from them. We had thunder, lightning, and rain. Armageddon was on my mind. Somebody had just said to me that Joan Baez was having a miscarriage. My dog was lost. My then-wife, Annie, had fallen and broken her ankle, and somebody said there was a guy in the audience with a gun. I had to keep the mike and therefore the electricity on because it was the only way to communicate with people. The mike was shorting out and I'm saying, "Move away from the towers. It will be okay. Everybody just hang on. We're going to ride this through. We've been through everything else." We offered them breakfast in bed, we told them the acts were going to be on, we had a symbiotic relationship at that point, and you couldn't walk out on them.

Then there were the accidents of when people played. Sha Na Na was shoved around and went on at dawn. And Eddie Goodgold, one of the nicer people on the face of the earth, was going bananas. He was their manager, and I just kept saying, "Ed, hang in there, it will work out." Sha Na Na lived another twenty years because of their performance at Woodstock.

Bill Belmont came to me and said, "Sly is not ready to go on. Sly doesn't feel the vibes." Well, at this point I didn't feel the vibes either. He was doing a star act. It wasn't a matter of being begged, he'd been begged. I looked at Belmont and we both said, "Do a Bill Graham." I grabbed Sly and lifted him up in the air, and said, "If you're not on stage in three minutes, I'm going to take your head off," and then I dropped him. He just looked at me. His eyes were the size of basketballs. He walked to the trailer and he said, "We're on." They went on and they did a fabulous show. All it was—and I learned that from working with Graham, God rest his soul, we all owe tremendous debts to Bill, not one of them being anger—but there were times when you could turn the thing around by acting. Because I literally dropped Sly, turned around, and looked at Belmont and smiled.

The Who were still not in love with the idea that Peter had been talked into doing this by Frank and me, and were quite exhausted and wanted to go home. Their manager, John Wolf, stormed me and said, "If we don't get paid before we go on, we're not going on," and I said, "It doesn't say anything in the contract about this." "It doesn't say anything in the contract about going on eight hours late in the rain, either," he said. So I picked up the phone and called John Roberts. It was about eleven o'clock at night and I said, "John, I need the Who's money." John got a bank officer out of bed to open the bank and put somebody on a motorcycle to bring me the money so the band could go on stage.

Joe MacDonald played the first solo performance

he'd ever played simply because, after Richie Havens, there was nobody else. I said, "Remember when we were in Amsterdam and we were talking about doing it on your own, please." I borrowed the first guitar I saw, slapped it into his hand, put my hand on the middle of his back, and shoved him on stage. He went out and was great. Those sorts of things happened.

Hendrix circled the festival for two days. We were unable to get him in and also to negotiate all the conditions that everybody wanted. Once Jimi actually went on stage, he was going to be the last act. It was four or five o'clock Monday morning, and I just went straight back to my trailer and laid down and went out like a light. I remember waking up hearing the first notes of "The Star-Spangled Banner."

I can honestly say I didn't have any drugs to assist me because I had enough adrenaline running to keep up half the world. I don't have any regrets about something that had such a great positive effect on me as a human being.

Transportation

LISA LAW   We were innocent flower children, living communally, sharing, playing music. We took mind-expanding drugs including marijuana. Music was taking a turn, expressing this new consciousness. Bob Dylan said, "The times they are a-changing." We all wanted to stop the war in Vietnam. Spiritual leaders were teaching the breath of fire and how to get in touch with our inner selves. We embraced the cultures of indigenous tribes, planted corn, lived in tepees that we made, and wore leather with fringe and beaded headbands. We were getting back to basics, rebelling against the status quo. We were "turning on, tuning in, and dropping out" and at the same time dropping back into society with a whole new twist: "Don't trash our Mother Earth, respect her. Be responsible human beings and come from a place of integrity and honesty."

In July 1969, Stan Goldstein, who was working for some promoters of a festival coming up in August, visited us at the Hog Farm in New Mexico. He was looking for a group of people to help him with the concert who had integrity and were part of the counterculture. We wanted to do it if we could do a free kitchen and take care of the fire trails, and Stan said we could. Volunteers from communes and local tribes poured down from the mountains of New Mexico, and we all crowded into buses for the ride to Albuquerque.

At the Albuquerque airport, while waiting for our jumbo jet to arrive, we took turns going to the bathroom to sip acid-tainted wine. Our tepee poles actually fit into the luggage compartment. During the flight the stewardesses were locked in the rest rooms, I think. Babies were running up and down the aisles.

At Kennedy Airport we were greeted by TV cameras and crews wanting to know if we were in charge of security. Wavy was shocked when he heard this, but he recovered quickly. "Do you feel secure?" he asked. "Yes," the reporter said. Then Wavy said, "See, it must be working." The news men hurriedly jotted it all down.

They ushered us into buses, and off we went to Bethel. Our buses, which had left New Mexico a week earlier, had arrived, and the crews were building the free stage. We put up a giant tepee that would be the PLEASE medical tent in our area, *please* being the word we used for "policing activities."

The advance crew had built a wooden dome, covered it with plastic, and set up a full kitchen. Max Yasgur provided us with milk, yogurt, and eggs. There was plenty of food, and we started feeding lines of early arrivals. These people were then given jobs helping to build forest trails and a jungle gym made out of logs and branches. A sandbox was constructed for kids.

Bonnie Jean Romney, Wavy's wife, was in charge of the kitchen and had gathered together pots and pans. We discussed just how much food would be needed and what we should serve. It was then that I realized (I do believe I got a direct message from God), that this was going to be bigger than any group we had fed before. We were going to need an immense amount of supplies.

Being well directed by the cosmic-powers-that-be, I approached John Morris and asked him for three thousand dollars. I guess I made a good case, as he gave me the cash with no hesitation, and to this day he tells the story of how I intimidated him more than anyone else in his life. Hog Farmer Peter White Rabbit and I pounded New York City streets for two days buying stainless-steel pots, utensils, and 160,000 paper plates. Then we ran out of money. The city festival office was just down the street. "Can I have another three thousand dollars?" I pleaded and went off again buying 1,500 pounds of bulgur wheat, 1,500 pounds of rolled oats, dried apricots, currants, honey, wheat germ, and huge kegs of soy sauce. In Chinatown I purchased a jade Buddha to protect and bless the kitchen.

We built a kitchen with lots of cutting and serving surfaces, and as soon as the five gas burners were set up, volunteers began to cook and never stopped until the concert was over. We made five serving booths that accommodated ten lines of people. For lunch and dinner we ate bulgur wheat with vegetables. Muesli was for breakfast, not very tasty but very nutritious. Being a health food nut, I figured nutrition was a major issue if one was going to be thrown against the elements. The elements showed up Friday night.

The stage was almost built and the fences were going up, but there were too many fences to be built and the turnstiles never got up. More and more people were camping out in the fields. They would walk right up to a fence, lay it down, and walk over it. Then they would plop themselves down on tarps, make a cushion of their sleeping bags, take off their tops to enjoy the sun, and stay there waiting for the music. There must have been fifty thousand of these squatters on the field by Friday morning. The promoters told my husband, Tom Law, and Wavy it was time to clear the fields and start taking tickets. Wavy said, "Do you want to have a good movie or a bad movie?" It became a free festival.

It was a tidal wave. People just kept coming. I stood up on top of the hill at the back of the stage and looked down the road and saw miles of cars parked at the shoulders of the road and six people abreast coming toward the field carrying clothes, coolers, and sleeping bags, big smiles on their faces.

What if all these people took acid at once? Yee gads! This could be a major problem. The Hogs got into a huddle and decided to put together a core of people who would take care of those tripsters in need. They would be recognized by red cloth armbands. By the end of the festival there must have been 200,000 people wearing the red armbands.

We helped medics set up their tents and erected "trip" tents next to theirs. If they got hold of a guy on acid, they would gingerly walk him to our tents instead of stopping his trip with Thorazine. Not good to stop in the middle, it can fuck with your reality the rest of your life. We shared with the tripster the fact that he was on a trip and would come down soon, which he did.

The free stage by the Hog Farm camp had its own music and audience. Some people never saw the main stage. Pup tents, tepees, and campers lined the hillsides.

The festival chiefs had hired off-duty police to help with traffic and crowd control. They wore T-shirts that read, PLEASE FORCE. It was supposed to establish peaceful security. It worked. Everyone was helping everyone else keep their scene together.

It rained Friday night and all throughout the festival, on and off. Fields became mud slides. It would start to pour, and people would stand up and let the water run through their feet. Then they would sit down again, not wanting to leave their place lest they lose it. Everyone was sharing their food. All the concessions started giving away their food, and the National Guard dropped supplies from planes. I would go to a neighboring farm

with a truck and buy whole rows of vegetables. Saturday morning after Tom Law taught yoga from the main stage, Wavy got up and said, "What we have in mind is breakfast in bed for four hundred thousand!" I then took the mike and told them where they could get this food. Realizing that lots of kids were not eating at all, we filled twenty-five new plastic trash cans with muesli mix and served it out of paper cups at the side of the stage along with cups of fresh water.

Once a day I would hail a helicopter, say I was with the Hog Farm, and get a lift into the sky. Yeaow, what a view! We had created our own city, half a million loving, sharing freaks. I could see the traffic for miles. People were still coming. Traffic was backed up all the way to the interstate. The lake behind the stage was filled with naked bathers. Helicopters were everywhere, dropping off and picking up performers who had no other way to get into the festival.

I ordered a truckload of food to come in from a neighboring town. It took the driver nine hours to drive the normal twenty-minute run. What could I say to him when he piled out of the truck in a rage? "Here, have some dinner on us and relax, and we thank you from the bottoms of our bellies."

Sleep was the farthest thing from my mind. I think I got one hour a day. On Sunday I got my first shower when the Hog Farmers rigged up a hose that someone would hold at the top of a ladder and aim down on the naked bodies below.

I know there was music at Woodstock. They said Crosby, Stills and Nash played their second gig there, that Santana wooed the crowd. Richie Havens created "Freedom" right on stage when he ran out of songs. Country Joe MacDonald got the crowd to yell out F-U-C-K, and Jimi Hendrix played the national anthem and made that guitar sing like no one else had ever done. But for me Woodstock was the people, getting along, sharing, caring, doctoring, feeding. It was the first time we were in charge, and we showed the world what life could be like. We had created the Woodstock Generation. "We could change the world, rearrange the world," Graham Nash wrote. Can that feeling ever be re-created? I would like to think so. That is why over twenty million people today will tell you they were at Woodstock.

Living Quarters

JOHN ROBERTS Joel and I met Michael Lang and Artie Kornfeld in February 1969 when we were building a recording studio in Manhattan. A lawyer by the name of Miles Lury called us up and said he had a couple of clients who were interested in building a recording studio in Woodstock, and he wondered if we would share our experiences with them.

The most important thing about organizing the festival was to get the right security. Wes Pomeroy was a decent, lovely gentleman. I guess that you'd describe him as a humanist, which was a surprise considering he came from a law enforcement background. In 1969 there were two schools of law enforcement. One was "Cuff 'em, book, 'em, take 'em to jail," and the other was "Reason with them, find out what their problems are." Wes definitely came from that second school.

We initially hoped that we would get a major player like Restaurant Associates to handle the food concessions. But as our problems mounted as we changed sites, responsible food purveyors had doubts as to whether we were going to pull this thing off. So finally a friend of a friend said there are these guys who have some food experience and they'd be interested in doing this, and I said anyone who'd bring truckloads of hot dogs up there would be great. So that's how we met Food for Love.

We spent a great deal of time conceptualizing what we wanted to do. We came up with the concept of peace and music. And *peace* was not intended as some kind of codeword for "get out of Vietnam." *Peace* was a shorthand way of saying "a weekend of freedom from whatever is bothering you. Just come to the country and have a nice time."

Max Yasgur had been following the accounts of our battles in Walkill, and when we were thrown out, he called us. Mel and Michael went up to look at the land and called me and said you've got to make a deal with this farmer. I hopped on my motorbike immediately. He was a delightful, charming guy, but he was also a businessman and he knew he had us over a barrel. We negotiated a deal with him for $50,000, plus we had to clean up. Max was an important person. He had a lot of good contacts, and since we felt we were going to generate some opposition once people realized what was going on, we moved forward with a surge of inevitability and hoped we might squeak through before the opposition could martial its forces and stop us. And that's in essence what happened.

We had one huge problem. We had sold about a million dollars' worth of tickets for Walkill, so we had to make sure everyone knew those tickets would be honored in White Lake. The press had been carrying accounts of how the festival was dead, so we had to counteract that. It was a nightmarish problem for roughly thirty days letting people who were confused know where the concert was going to be.

After the festival I was at the bank in New York talking to a bunch of panicked bankers when I got a call that a dead body had been found when they were cleaning up. The guy had been accidentally run over by the machinery that was compacting and gathering the trash. It was pretty emotional. Joel and I were both in the bank, and it felt like our world had collapsed. We had spent well in excess of a million dollars over the receipts, the newspaper accounts of Woodstock the morning after were not friendly, the *Times* had headlined it, NIGHTMARE IN THE CATSKILLS . We had bankers and creditors and just about everyone breathing down our necks and then the information that this boy had been killed accidentally at the site felt like the last straw. I remember feeling broken up about it.

The bank said they'd paid out a million dollars over the original $250,000 we had in our account but had no documentation to support it. We said it was our intention to honor these debts and we would sign whatever papers were necessary. That was something that my father had always felt strongly about. You can regain lost money, but lost reputations are forever.

If we had had the hundred thousand people we were expecting, that would have been twenty to thirty thousand cars and we probably could have handled that without too much trouble because we had hundreds of acres of parking lots. But we had four to five times as many people, so we had many more cars. Also it rained, so many of the parking lots were a sea of mud. You couldn't drive in there.

We started getting reports that the surrounding community was very upset about long hair, drugs, what have you. You have to go back to 1969 and recall the temper of the times. People under twenty-five with long hair were widely suspected of all kinds of unnatural behavior by people over twenty-five with short hair, and we felt we didn't want to fuel those fires. So one of the things we asked people constructing the site was that they not use drugs and that they comport themselves in ways designed to reassure the local people.

What I recall vividly is around one o'clock Friday morning Joel and I decided to take a ride to visit the parking areas. Most of them were empty. At some point we crested a hill on our motorbikes. I can remember just looking out over the hills toward where the festival was and all I could see were campfires. I had the sense of this massive army before the battle, waiting there. And it reminded me of *Henry V*. It was a still, misty evening. Joel and I looked at each other with this—what's that great expression that Keats has?—with "a look of wild surmise." What does all this mean for us and what will the morrow bring? It was a wonderful moment that I'll always remember.

The Yasgurs were decent, gentle, caring people. They came to our rescue. There would have been no Woodstock without Max and Miriam Yasgur. When the festival was over and there was all this trouble because of the dead boy, the lawsuits, the pillaring in the press, and the loss of money, the Yasgurs were steadfast friends. They didn't call up and say, "You didn't clean up this or that acre, you didn't do this or that," but "Anything we can do to help?" We did clean up their land. Max called me a month after the festival and said, "I can imagine what you're going through, I know you're only twenty four years old. You must be having a nightmare of a time. I have a great idea, why don't you come up here for a month and milk cows. You can forget about Woodstock for a month." I almost took him up on it, but I had met a girl at Woodstock, and my romance took precedence over milking cows. I married her.

From there Joel and I stayed in the music business; we remained and still are partners. We ran that recording studio and production company for the next ten years. We have been in the venture-capital business ever since. We are not really button-down types. We've gotten involved in dozens of strange, interesting ventures over the years. In fact things have come full circle—we're producing a twenty-fifth anniversary event in 1994. The world has changed a lot, and there are a lot of roadblocks in our way. But it's got a shot. (Note: John Roberts has been married for 24 years to a woman he connected with at Woodstock. Tara Roberts, author of the following memoir, is not related to him.)

TARA ROBERTS   Woodstock, long before the tourists and music, had a very big beat population. I remember growing up in the early sixties, Woodstock had guys hanging out on the street with no shirts and long hair and beads back when it was like really weird to see people like that. We grew up living next door to Bob Dylan and we would go over and and listen to him jamming with Joan Baez, Jimi Hendrix, and Janis Joplin. We didn't have the foggiest idea who they were, but we enjoyed the music. Years later, in 1969, when I was twelve, I had a summer job working behind the counter at Cary's Deli. I asked my mom if I could go to the Woodstock Festival. She said no and that was the end of that. It was sixty miles away, but droves of kids came in, asking where the festival was, where they were going to sleep and eat, and where the bathrooms were. We didn't have bathrooms, free food, or free places to sleep, so there were all these kids with nowhere to go and no money. Lucky for me I worked for a very generous lunatic and we just fed people until we were out of food. When the kids came in and didn't have money, we gave them sandwiches and stuff for free or for discounts, like a nickle. After the festival, we had a really high population of teenage runaways, so some people began Family to take care of the problem.

It seems to me that the festival idea started from Saturday-night sound-ins that were held at Pam Copland's field. We'd go and see all of those old rock greats jamming and playing, Janis Joplin, Bob Dylan, Jimi Hendrix, and Richie Havens. I really remember Jimi Hendrix and Janis Joplin most because their music was so intense. Michael Lang wanted to do the festival in Woodstock, but the local noise ordinance stopped it from happening here.

Even though Woodstock had not been known before the sixties as a place where music was coming from, it had always been a place of alternative lifestyles. It was also a well-known arts colony. All of Byrdcliffe was housing for artists, and the rents were made affordable for them. Classical musicians and composers would come into Woodstock in the summer and work at the Maverick concerts. So you had this group of artists, musicians, poets, and composers.

I think that the festival was a natural metamorphosis of all of Woodstock's history—an accumulation of free and progressive thinkers and creative people.

People

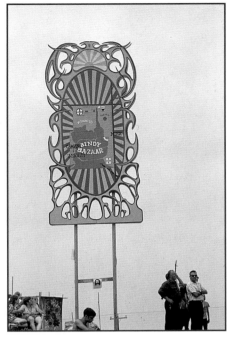

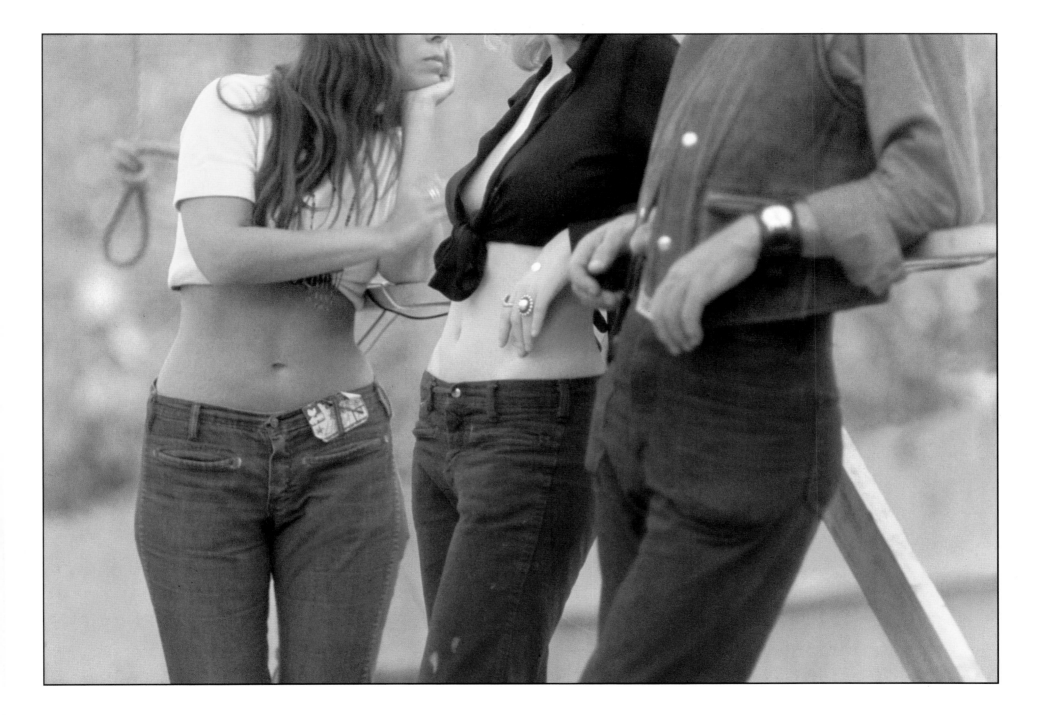

Joe Cocker

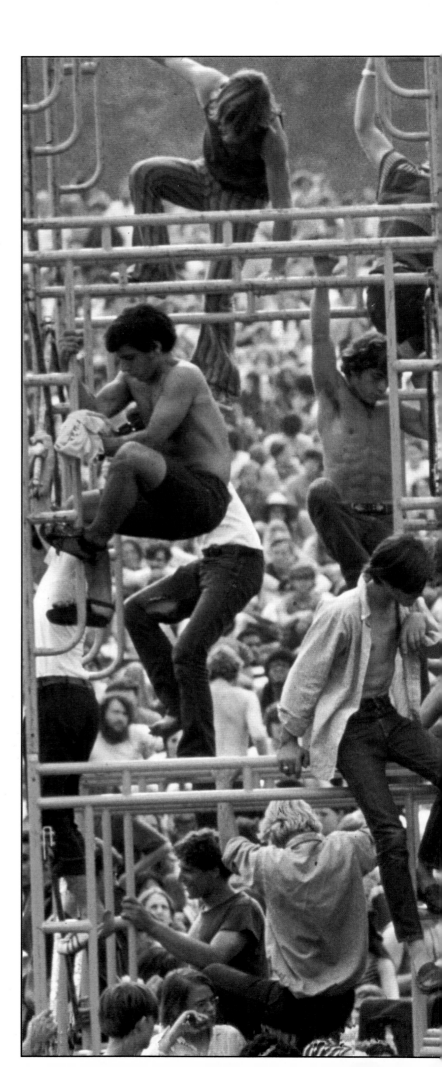

BARBARA RISSMAN   We noticed these big full-page ads in *The New York Times* that said, "Three days of peace and music, at the Woodstock Festival." All these great musicians were going to be there. I was eighteen and had just graduated high school, and my friends and I really wanted to go. Of course we didn't have tickets. I told my parents that I was going to a concert in the Catskills and they said, "Fine, have a good time." We drove up there. The traffic was so backed up, we had to stop and leave our car on the thruway. It was miles from the concert, so we just hopped on the roof of a car that was allowed to go through and just inched along having a great time.

We arrived that Friday night. It was pretty dark and we had missed the first night of the concert. There was just a field there, and we decided to put our sleeping bags down and go to sleep. We woke up in the middle of the night, as it was raining pretty hard and we were soaked. We had to find shelter. We saw a barn in the distance and headed toward it. When we got up there, there was a whole bunch of people hanging out, and they were really welcoming. They said, "Oh, come on in, there's room." They had food and they shared it with us. In the morning when we got up, the farmer was very nice. He came out and said, "You kids are welcome to stay and use the barn." He allowed us to use the bathrooms in the house and use the telephones to call our parents collect, and so I did and said everything was fine.

That morning we went to the concert grounds. The crowds of people everywhere were just unbelievable. There were babies running around naked and babies on their parents' shoulders, and there were drugs everywhere. People were passing joints around. I remember being warned about brown acid, but mostly there was a real feeling of warmth and connection between all the people. There were people selling things like jewelry, and people bathing in a stream and waterfalls. It was just wonderful being there.

During the day I remember seeing Joe Cocker playing, and then there was a big rainstorm and we all went for shelter. But Saturday night was beautiful. During the concert we were walking through crowds of people to get closer to the stage. It was so muddy that we sank down into mud up to our ankles. I remember taking my shoes off because mud was gushing inside them and it was very uncomfortable. It didn't matter, because my feet felt warm and squishy and it was fine.

Creedence Clearwater played, and it was sort of warming up, and the Who played, and things were getting hotter and hotter, and then when Sly and the Family Stone played, everyone was jumping up and saying, "I want to take you higher." The whole experience was about warmth and friendliness. Whoever had food just passed it around. Joints got passed around, and there was this very good feeling. If you said, "Excuse me," and wanted to get up closer, nobody said, "Hey, I'm here first." Everybody was very polite.

Crosby, Stills and Nash played, and that was great. Then Janis Joplin, and we were sitting so close that you could see the beads of sweat flying off her as she sang, and it was incredible. When the Who played, they were throwing and breaking their instruments on stage, and the fringes on Peter Townshend's jacket were incredible.

No one slept, we went right through the whole night until dawn. Then as the morning came, Jefferson Airplane played. All these groups played as the sun was coming up, and it was really amazing.

Later we headed back toward the barn, but by this time there was no plumbing at all in the whole area. The farmer no longer could let us use the bathrooms. The whole area was overtaxed. The phones were dead. I don't think we brought food of our own, but it really wasn't a problem, because there was food. The Hog Farm was serving meals.

I spoke to and met people from all over the country. It was at that time that I realized that I had other possibilities, that I could've gone off to California. There was this feeling that you really didn't need money. I don't know how much I had with me, probably not more than twenty-five dollars. But somehow there was a feeling that you'd make it, that you'd be fine, and that you could really do something else and have a real adventure.

Sunday there was another great concert, and we spent the whole day there. Then, Monday morning, everybody had cleared out, but we heard some music. The barn wasn't that far from the field, so we walked up there. The field was now this vast open space, and there was just garbage strewn about. But when we got close,

Jimi Hendrix was playing, and that was really amazing. I found a Woodstock book lying on the ground among the rubble, and I still have it today.

I had a fantastic time, it was a highlight of my life, one of the most wonderful experiences I have had. I was so happy that I went. Driving home, we were all so exhilarated and high, not from drugs but just from having been part of this experience. I haven't been back to Yasgur's farm since, but I now live in Woodstock.

That afternoon when I came home, my parents were frantic. They had been in a panic because they had been watching the news and they heard that Woodstock was declared a national disaster area, that people were dying, that there wasn't enough food, no plumbing, and there were all these drugs. My father was a dentist, and he said that he'd been working on a patient who said, "Any parent who let their kid go there should be shot." And my father said he just kept his mouth shut. My mother said, "You know, when you said you were going to a concert in the Catskills, I thought it was something like Tanglewood. I thought you were going to be having a picnic on the lawn." The media highlighted certain aspects, the death, the people who were having bad trips on acid, the mud. I realized how things could be really peaceful with everybody sharing a common goal but it would be portrayed very differently by the press. So my parents were very upset that I had gone, but I was elated. I'll always remember Woodstock.

WES POMEROY   In 1968 I was training chiefs of police how to deal with riot prevention and control. I went to Washington because Ramsey Clark asked me to be his special assistant. I had picked up a law degree at night school, so I was qualified for a Department of Justice job.

I finally resigned and started Pomeroy Associates. Not too long afterward Stan Goldstein came to see me to talk about a Woodstock festival he was involved with. After making sure the promoters had ideas that I agreed with about keeping the peace and that they expected no guns or billyclubs, I said, "I'll work with you." I didn't know I'd end up running it.

Of course Woodstock is a lot of things to a lot of people. It's several things to me too. But one thing it was, was a real test of logistical planning and implementation and coordination of some key things that we needed to have happen with some good people doing it.

The one thing that surprised me, and pleasantly so, was that I was the oldest guy in the whole thing, and at forty-nine years old I saw these young guys in their twenties who obviously knew so much. I very quickly learned to respect them for what they could do. They did incredible things.

Michael Lang was the first one I met. He was a very interesting guy. I'd met some people like him before, people who were beginning to say, "If it feels right, it's right." And I had come to respect that. I hadn't really adopted it myself, but I understood it.

John and Joel looked like establishment guys, but they obviously had enough vision and adventure to go along with this, because they were taking a hell of a risk, particularly John, because it was his money. I saw they knew what they were talking about. I could see as they developed things, they were right on top of everything. I liked them both.

My fee was two hundred dollars a day and it looked like it might be a very interesting experience. However, it was important for me not to blow my career on what someone may have seen as a hippie adventure. After people got used to it, it didn't bother anybody much, except I'm sure I had a file with the FBI.

We began recruiting New York City police officers to work at the festival. They wouldn't be carrying weapons and they would be wearing a uniform that looked peaceful and not militant. We showed them the bellbottom jeans and the red shirt with the peace sign on the front and the dove on the back. We hired about 335 of them.

Just a few days before the concert the police commissioner of New York said no policemen could go. That caused some consternation. However, we had the Hog Farm, who had some very creative ideas concerning security. We also had cops who came up anyway and were willing to work but wouldn't give their names.

You know, I get a lot of kudos for the security, but everybody was working on security, the whole environment, it was all part of an interwoven dynamic.

After it was over, I would have liked to stay for another week, because we had a lot of cleaning up to do and we were just getting started.

John had really gone way over his credit line, and the manager of the local bank was so distraught, we were afraid he was going to commit suicide because he had extended so much credit to us. We had people coming in saying, "I have ten acres here and people have been tromping all over it," and we'd say, "What kind of crop did you have?" By the time we got through, we knew how to estimate an acre of alfalfa or corn. We were paying them off for as long as we had money. But the last money we had went to pay the doctors.

We had to reassure those who had worked for us, "We know who you are and you're going to be taken care of, don't worry." I was pretty confident that what I said was true. I didn't know how John was going to do it, but my assessment of him was that he would take care of folks he promised to pay, and he did.

DODEE GIEBAS (*Dodee, the girl dancing on page 64, wrote the following piece.*) I feel fortunate to have been part of that experience. A movement, started in the sixties, crystallized at that time and place. I will carry it in my heart and soul forever.

It was advertised as three days of peace and music—and it was. People came from all over North America, from the East Coast to the West Coast. I went with a group of thirty people from Pittsburgh. We rented a thirty-foot U-Haul and lined the inside with old mattresses. At twenty I was the oldest of the group and one of the only two girls.

After driving all night we spent our first day in the Woodstock vicinity in a traffic jam leading up to the grounds. It became a giant, slow-moving road party in a country setting. We could hear the music plainly five miles away. The acoustics were amazing, since the stage was built in a pasture where the land formed a bowl, a natural amphitheater. Many people got out of their crowded vehicles and continued to the site on foot. Our huge, comfortable truck attracted many fans for a visit, and we shared whatever sustenance they may have had. We began to make new friends.

By the time we reached the festival grounds, the gate was down, and it was declared a free concert! We parked our truck in a field by an old hay barn. If it became too hot in the truck, we planned to camp in the hayloft. I never even saw the inside of that barn because my friend and I decided to camp in the rain directly in front of center stage. We told our group to meet us there in the morning. Our night was spent sitting on two sleeping bags in the mud, shivering as the cool rain fell. The fire we built of wood and pieces of trash was a small comfort.

In the morning we spread out our sleeping bags to hold our spot, and soon our friends began to arrive. The concert began again and went almost continuously for the next two days. I stayed in that spot for the duration, only leaving when necessary and once to cool off in a nearby pond.

I can't speak for everyone at Woodstock, but my group was there for the music. We were the "counterculture," the "underground," and the music was our voice. The musicians were our champions, chosen by us to sing of our ideals and lifestyle. We had everything from Country Joe and the Fish singing, "Give me an F, give me a U," et cetera, to Joan Baez's beautiful rendition of "Amazing Grace." Country Joe also sang in protest of the Vietnam War. We had Richie Havens crying out for "Freedom," a powerful song, and Joe Cocker getting by and getting high with "a little help from my friends." Canned Heat sang about getting back to basics, "going to the country where the water tastes like wine."

And of course, being the outcasts of society that we were, we all related to the blues that were played for us by Ten Years After, Paul Butterfield Blues Band, the great Johnny Winter, and the always fantastic Janis Joplin. There was also good listening music by Santana, a favorite of mine. Some was more entertaining, such as Arlo Guthrie's story of Alice's Restaurant.

The Who played their complete rock opera, *Tommy*. They were the last group to play on the second day of the festival, and when Tommy triumphed at the end of the opera, the sun was rising behind the stage—very dramatic. Steam was rising off the drummer. All the bands played their hearts out for us; we, in our massive number, provided the ultimate gratification for them.

Drugs were a part of our lifestyle; there were songs about the drug experience. The Grateful Dead gave "High on Cocaine," and Jefferson Airplane offered their haunting "White Rabbit." We heard Jimi Hendrix's "Purple Haze," about lovin' life on LSD, "'Scuse me while I kiss the sky."

Yes, we used drugs; many abused drugs. Some took drugs just to "party." Others used drugs to escape the reality they couldn't face. Some of us were on a spiritual quest for the truth, and we used drugs as a means of breaking away the bonds of a false personality imposed upon us by society and our parents—a search for the essence of our being, not having found it in structured religion. But we found there was a price to pay for using drugs, and payment was extracted from us mentally and physically. Many couldn't afford to pay the price, and some lost their sanity or their lives.

But not at Woodstock! For those three days we triumphed. We were the counterculture, a minority, but at Woodstock we were half a million strong. We proved to ourselves and to the world that people can coexist in peace and harmony under the most adverse conditions. We withstood a seven-mile traffic jam, a severe electrical storm, intense heat and humidity, a shortage of food and water, lack of sleep, overcrowding, a lack of facilities—in a sea of mud there were smiles on our faces. Never before or since have I seen so many ear-to-ear grins. There was not one act of violence in the three days of Woodstock. Can you grasp the enormity of that?

You may or may not be familiar with the Greek concept of *agape*. It means selfless, unconditional, nonsexual love—universal love. It was present at Woodstock, I know, I was there, I felt it surrounding me. At one point a helicopter dropped thousands of daisies from the sky. The daisies twirled down, their little heads spinning like propellers. We caught them. Thousands of us stood with daisies in our hands. We were the "flower children" and it was our symbol—a symbol of gentleness and beauty. Incredible!

Hamburgers were also dropped from a helicopter. There weren't enough for everyone, so we shared. In fact everything was shared by all throughout the festival. It just happened that way. Whatever came your way, you took a bite or a sip of and passed it on. If you focused on one thing such as a sandwich, you could see it growing smaller as it zigzagged through the crowd. If there was a jug of wine, the level receded as it bobbed on its way. I had a variety of things come my way. I can remember a dill pickle, I took a bite and passed it on; marijuana, sandwiches, apples, beer, wine, water, soda. I wasn't hungry or thirsty the entire time I was there.

Every once in a while someone would strip and run through the crowd in a celebration of life and freedom; we thought it beautiful. Imagine—no embarrassment or false modesty, just love of life in its purest form. There was one guy who walked unclothed for two days carrying a sheep. He had a sign on his back: "Don't eat animals. They're our friends." An outsider probably would have viewed us as a dirty, sweaty mass of half-naked, drug-crazed hippies. We were "hip." I've been attempting to explain what that meant and what it felt like to be there, a part of the whole. It was beautiful, it was awesome, it was incredible. I kept thinking, "This can't really be happening. It's too good to be true. It must be a dream and I'm going to wake up."

We went to Woodstock for the music, and although the music was phenomenal, we found so much more—memories and good feelings to last a lifetime.

After Woodstock many of us became disillusioned. Some chose to drown themselves in drugs; I chose to travel in search of life's mysteries. I leaped naked off of sand dunes on the beach at Big Sur. I stayed alone in a tepee on a mountaintop in the foothills of the Canadian Rockies. I cruised in the ocean with the dolphins from Maine to Nova Scotia. I body-surfed in the warm Caribbean off the coast of Puerto Rico. I danced in the surf in the moonlight and watched the sun rise from a desert island in the Keys. My brother was a diabetic—I watched him die by inches. I saw how much you lose if you lose your health.

After years I realized that the world isn't ready for world peace or world government or even ecological appreciation. Humanity has not yet evolved to that level. The love I felt at Woodstock was a microcosm of future possibilities. My generation pointed the way; it's up to future generations to try to take us back to the Garden.

I decided to make the most of what the world had to offer. At twenty-nine I had a child. I then needed a career and went back to school at thirty-three. It was one of the most difficult challenges of my life. I finished second in a class of young, aggressive, competitive males in a male-dominated field, a major personal triumph.

Today I live with my family in wild and wonderful West Virginia in the country near the Potomac River.

Bill Graham

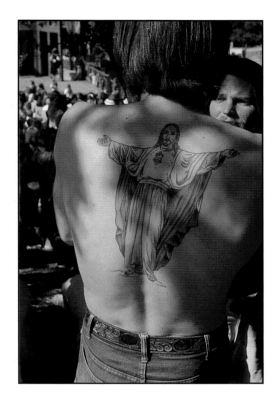

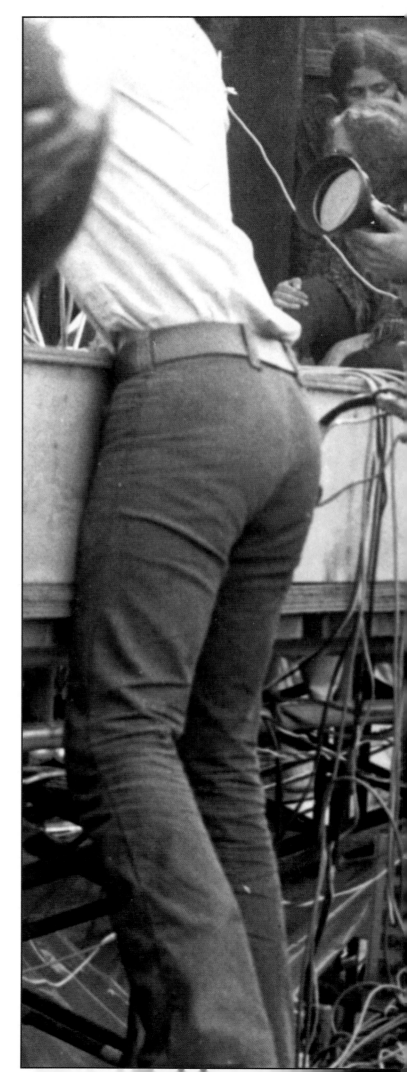

Ameni ties

HENRY DILTZ   The first pictures I took of Woodstock were of Mel Lawrence looking at the rain out the window and talking on the telephone calling contractors. From there I followed him around. I saw where they were going to put the water pipes, where people would be camping, having booths and concession stands. We walked through the woods to where the Hog Farm was going to be. This was all before anyone had arrived; it was just Mel and me walking through these green fields of alfalfa.

A few days later the Hog Farm arrived, and they set up their tepees and cook shacks. In the afternoons after work when it got real hot, they'd jump into their multicolored school bus and go swimming. Men, women, and lots of little kids would take off all their clothes and jump in the lake, about sixty of them.

The stage was under construction. There were hippie guys hammering nails with their shirts off, and there was this beautiful hill with waving green grass, alfalfa blowing in the wind, and blue sky. It was really beautiful.

At this point there was no urgency. It was like being at summer camp, just an idyllic summer afternoon in upstate New York. Hippie ladies would come in the afternoon with sandwiches and drinks for lunch for everyone, and they'd have a big picnic on the stage deck.

My job was to hang out and take pictures. I'd follow the art people around while they were painting big banners, and then I'd watch people do the wiring and carpentry. Everyone seemed busy but not frantic.

When the rain came, there was chaos. Everybody had ponchos on, trucks were getting stuck in the mud. Then the weather was nice for a long stretch of time.

I'd be taking pictures, and Michael Lang would come along on a motorcycle, a horse, or a tractor. Every time he'd have his leather vest on with his curly hair, and he was always very positive. Any time you'd ask him a question, he'd say, "Right, go for it, sure, fine." Everything was very pleasant, nobody was uptight, nobody was shouting orders, nobody was tense about anything. It was a real neat vibe.

Then things changed suddenly one afternoon. There was a small group of people sitting in this previously empty field. What were they doing here, watching us build? During the afternoon the crowd got a little larger, until there was quite a sizable group of people sitting there, and then you started to think, "Wait a minute, these people are here for the concert, and here we are, we're not even ready for them yet." Suddenly there was that feeling.

I made a trip to my boardinghouse in my station wagon. I didn't know it was going to be my last trip, but luckily I brought all my film back and I parked behind the stage. The following day I tried to go back to my room, but I couldn't, because the roads were totally plugged with cars. Cars would park on the shoulders of the road, so there was no way to go around. The roads became parking lots.

As the concert went on, it became hard to get on the stage, even though I had an access pass. If I would leave the stage for an hour to go photograph something else, by the time I came back, that pass was no good anymore, unless it had the purple star on it, say, and then you had to run off and find the right person to give you the purple star, all of which took a lot of time. There were just so many people on the stage, they had to clear them off and just change the passes. The best place to take photos was right from the side of the stage, which was where I spent most of my time. I remember shooting Richie Havens, John Sebastian, and Joe Cocker. It was terrific to be there on stage able to shoot all those people.

There was panic on stage when the winds were whipping up, since they were whipping these canvas things that they had tied up. It was like a ship with a storm suddenly coming on and the guys quickly furling the sails. Guys were scrambling around trying to cover amps and take down things that were in danger of blowing away, and everyone was hurriedly putting on ponchos, and then the rain came. It didn't really seem to affect the audience much—they just stayed there. At one point a bunch of the crew walked out to the edge of the stage and heaved beer cans into the audience, and I stood right next to them taking pictures. As I stood on the lip of the stage, I could see people for 180 degrees, the people went on forever—a sea of faces.

Jimi Hendrix played into the dawn the last day. A lot of people had left, but there was still a sizable crowd. It was a sea of mud. Belongings that had been left behind, parts of tents, blankets, soggy sleeping bags, paper, garbage everywhere. It looked like a Civil War battlefield. It went on for acres and acres. What had once been a beautiful hillside of blowing grass was just a mud hole.

When it was over, I was concerned about this huge bag of film. Nobody knew this was going to be a famous thing until we were right in the middle of it and saw the headlines in *The New York Times* and saw the aerial photographs. I remember racing into New York City, developing my film at a photo lab, and taking it to *Life* magazine.

GREIL MARCUS   The police estimated that there were a million people on the road that day trying to get to the festival. A million people. 168,000 tickets had been sold, and the promoters figured that maybe 200,000 tops would show. That seemed outlandish, if believable. But no one was prepared for what happened, and no one could have been.

Perhaps a quarter of a million never made it. They gave up and turned back, or parked on the highway and set up tents on the divider strip and stuck it out. Shit, they'd come to camp out for three days and they were gonna do it. Many had walked fifteen miles in the rain and the mud, only to give up a mile or so before the festival and turn back, but they were having fun. Camped on the highway with no idea where White Lake was or what was going on, they were digging it, making friends, dancing to car radios and making their own music on their own guitars.

"Isn't it pretty here, all the trees and the meadows? And whenever it gets too hot, it rains and cools everyone off. Wow." "Yeah, sure, but you paid eighteen dollars and drove all the way from Ohio and you can't even get to the festival. Aren't you disappointed? Or pissed off?" "No, man. Everyone is so friendly, it's like being stuck in an elevator with people when the power goes off. But it's much nicer here than in an elevator."

It was an amazing sight, the highway to White Lake. It looked, as someone said, like Napoleon's army retreating from Moscow. It looked like that for three days. Everywhere one saw tents and campfires, cars rolled into ditches, people walking, lying down, drinking, eating, reading, singing. Kids were sleeping, making love, wading in the marshes, trying to milk the local cows, and trying to cook the local corn. The army of New York State Quickway 17B was on maneuvers.

***

Crosby, Stills and Nash opened with "Judy Blue Eyes," stretching it out for a long time, exploring the figures of the song for the crowd, making their quiet music and flashing grimaces at each other when something went wrong. They strummed and picked their way through other numbers and then began to shift around, Crosby singing with Stills, then Nash and Crosby, back and forth. They had the crowd all the way. Many have remarked that their music is perfect, but sterile; that night it wasn't quite perfect and it was anything but sterile. They seemed like several bands rather than one.

After perhaps half an hour Neil Young made his way into the band and sat down with Steve Stills, and the two of them combined for an extraordinary acoustic version of "Mr. Soul." Stills pushed stinging blues out of his guitar, and Young's singing was as disturbing and compelling as ever. And from that point they just took off. They switched to rock and roll and a grateful electricity—Nash, Stills, Crosby and /or Young on guitar, Young and Stills trading off on organ, and two terrific sidemen, Dallas Taylor on drums and Greg Reeves on bass.

Visually they are one of the most exciting bands I have ever seen, the six of them. David Crosby finally looks exactly like Buffalo Bill, his flowing hair and twisted mustaches twirling in the lights. Steve Stills, from Canada (it was a night for Canadians), seemed as Californian as a beach boy, with pageboy blond hair, a Mexican serape fitting the Baja Peninsula groove he's so fond of. Graham Nash appeared as one of these undernourished-in-childhood English kids, weighing in at maybe seventy-five pounds. And Neil Young, as usual, looked like a photo from Agee's *Let Us Now Praise Famous Men*, Dust Bowl Gothic, huge bones hung with very little flesh, all shaped by those odd, piercing eyes that have warmth even as they show fear. And Taylor! This is a drummer. He plays his stuff like P. J. Proby sings, shaking his head wildly—the most cataclysmic drummer I've ever seen. Well, they hit it. Right into "Long Time Gone," a song for a season if there ever was one, Stills on organ, shouting out the choruses, Neil snapping out the lead, Crosby aiming his electric twelve-string out over the edge of the stage, biting off his words and stretching them out, those lyrics that are as strong as any we are likely to hear. I have never seen a musician more involved in his music. At one point Crosby nearly fell off the stage in his excitement.

Deep into the New York night they were, early Sunday morning in the dark after three days of chaos and order, and it seemed like the last of a thousand and one American nights. Two hundred thousand people covered the hills of a great natural amphitheater, campfires burning in the distance, the lights shining down from the enormous towers onto the faces of the band. Crosby, Stills, Nash and Young were just one of the many at this festival, and perhaps they wouldn't top the bill if paired with Hendrix or the Airplane or Creedence Clearwater or the Who or The Band, but this was a scary, brilliant proof of the magnificence of music, and I don't believe it could have happened with such power anywhere else. This was a festival that had triumphed over itself, as Crosby and his band led the way toward the end of it.

the Music

Joe Cocker's band

Max Yasgur w.
Martin Scorcese
returning the
peace sign

Grace Slick

Leslie West, Mountain

Canned Heat

The Grateful Dead

Alvin Lee, Ten Years After
→

Graham Nash, David Crosby

Stephen Stills

Neil Young

David Crosby

CROSBY, STILLS, NASH & YOUNG

Ravi Shankar

Arlo Guthrie

John Sebastian

Melanie

Richie Havens

Joe Cocker

Jefferson Airplane

Sly Stone

Tim Hardin

Ten Years After

Johnny Winter

The Who

Roger Daltry

Roger Daltry

Pete Townshend

Joan Baez

Sly & the
Family Stone
band member

Janis Joplin

Jimi Hendrix

MICHAEL LANG   Woodstock was very much like we hoped it would be but much bigger. A lot of the work we did was to make sure that the feeling, once you arrived, was very much like what happened. We spent time making sure that things that were going wrong with other shows didn't go wrong with ours. I went to other events and saw the problems. There were a lot of riots, and I saw that they were always setups by the security, and preplanned confrontations, and it seemed really senseless to me. It was Stanley Goldstein's idea to have the Hog Farm as security, great idea.

We intended Woodstock to be a social statement. We designed it as a gathering of the tribes. We were trying to get all of the bands that had any relevance that year, and all of the people that you recognized every place that you went in the country, to come together and more or less see if they could live the idea—the dream. And it came pretty close.

In what way didn't it come close?

Monday morning everybody went back to their former lives, but I think everybody carried something with them that they probably carry to this day—which was the knowledge that you can have that kind of feeling, that sense of community, that sense of togetherness with a massive amount of people that you really didn't know before. I think it gave everybody a lot of hope.

There were lots of things that made it special, but I think it was all born out of that same sense of community, the part of you that acts with helping your neighbor, pulling together, and dealing with natural adversities with a sense of community.

There was such an amazing feeling in the air, you could feel it on the thruway, you could feel it on the roads leading to this thing, you could feel it for miles and miles. So much positive energy in one spot is an awesome thing.

We designed the festival so the music was no more or less important than any other element. The people were the stars, and bands are made up of people, so music was very much a part of it but no bigger part than anything else. The music was billed alphabetically so there were no stars. We really meant to focus on the whole event, not on any one thing, and that worked really well for us.

What was it like at age twenty-four, being the organizer and having to be responsible for getting so many things done on an impossible schedule?

I had a great time. It was a chance to live out a dream—to make it a reality. It was a great experience for me. I guess I knew how all the pieces fit together, because I had an overview of it. You have to deal with the problems one by one, and not get too excited, otherwise you don't get through them. It's my nature to do whatever there is to be done. If you see things that are being left undone, you do them.

What were the best and worst things that happened?

The best thing that happened was everything that happened. The worst thing was the financial mess afterward, and the fact that the four of us who did Woodstock were really too young and immature to deal with it well. There was a lot of financial pressure, and it took a long time to work out.

Did you realize what was happening when it was happening? Did you realize it was going to last twenty-five years?

Well, you don't think in those terms, but you realized that something very extraordinary was happening, everybody realized that.

Did you fully realize your vision?

Yes, completely. We didn't go into it wanting to lose money, but in every other aspect it was certainly everything we wanted it to be.

Jerry Garcia wrote in the introduction to this book that it was like there was an extraterrestial presence at Woodstock.

Certainly a great spirit was watching over that site. Woodstock was definitely cosmic and magical.

ELLIOTT LANDY   On August 15, 16, and 17, 1969, nearly 500,000 people gathered together to celebrate life. They came looking for music and new ways. They found a hard path—there were miles to walk, rain and mud, not much food to eat nor shelter to sleep beneath; life was not as they usually knew it.

But something happened. There was peace and harmony despite conditions that might have set off riots. Most everyone lived in consideration and enjoyment with everyone else.

Woodstock became a symbol to the world of a better way of life—of freedom, of love, of spiritual union between many. There was hope.

Twenty years have passed. "What has happened? Where has Woodstock gone?" Words are heard: "It was a fluke." "It can never happen again." "It was not real."

The coming of a new consciousness is a slow process. Woodstock is a way of thinking, a way of being—kindness, consideration, sharing and enjoying; life as it should be and would be if we lived that way.

Astrologically the birth of the age of Aquarius is upon us—an age of peace and understanding, a golden age. Like all births, the birth of this new consciousness is difficult.

Old ways are falling away as new ways evolve. The time of labor nears. A soft seedling must break through a hard seed shell. A baby comes through a birth, which can be painful.

Change is often difficult, but what is outside the new door is usually better than what was behind the old. Our habits are given by the culture we grow up in, the physical realities of our planet, and the needs we have. With the coming of new, clean technologies, physical wants can be met— people no longer have to fight to survive. There can be enough for everyone.

Woodstock showed us that people can live together in a peaceful and sharing way. It showed that the goal many were going toward during those years was reachable. It actually happened for 500,000 people at one time for three days.

The mystical teachings tell us that with the birth of each age there is a sign, a teacher, that appears, to lead the way. As Christ was the example for a world two thousand years ago, so the experience at Woodstock can be an example for our world today. Just as the birth of Jesus could find no place, so, too, Woodstock was without welcome—yet both found their destined place to be—one in Bethlehem, the other in Bethel, the similarity of names whispering to us of a cosmic declaration, an intelligence beyond our own.

The festival was like a conception. Now the cells are busy dividing and multiplying—separately and together, in nearby and faraway places. It was a cosmic sign—both symbolic and actual—telling us that our ideals could be made real, that a new time was approaching, telling us to keep on trying. And it is still, many years later, telling us that.

Waste Management

ALLEN GORDON   I was drawn to live in Woodstock in 1967 because it was where Bob Dylan lived. Woodstock was becoming a mecca for the culture of the mid-60's. The Vietnam War, electronic transformation, and psychedelics were altering people's consciousness on a mass scale, and a lot of people were drawn to alternate lifestyles.

I met Michael Lang in Coconut Grove, Florida, where he owned the Head Shop. It was a time when people were being profoundly changed from what had been another way of looking at life that was more linear and materialistic. The Vietnam War created a great wave of protest in this country, and the desire to throw off a lot of the old values led to a collective feeling of love.

I went to see Michael about three weeks before the festival and asked him if I could get a ticket for the festival. I was very broke in those days. He said, "Sure, come down." I drove over, and he gave me a ticket, and I felt so lucky. We thought maybe fifty thousand people were going to come. I came there a week before the festival with three or four dozen people from Woodstock, who helped the Hog Farm set up the free kitchen. There was the Ohayo Mountain Commune, Robert DePew Reynolds, Chris Grodon, a whole cluster of people that were living in this nude psychedelic commune on the top of Ohayo Mountain, hidden way back off the road in a building owned by Jerry Shultz, the owner of Slugs in New York City.

Everybody sensed something big was about to happen, but no one knew the enormity of it. The town itself was burgeoning with music. I remember one night in Woodstock, Santana was at the Elephant Cafe, Van Morrison was singing at the Sled Hill Cafe, Johnny Winter was playing at the Cafe Espresso. Just before the festival Jimi Hendrix was practicing "The Star-Spangled Banner" at the Tinker Street Cinema and he sang that at the festival. Odetta was in town, and Paul Butterfield was playing. I said, "God, look at this amazing place we're living in." I felt very privileged to be a part of this cultural renaissance.

I had a spiritual revelation, I saw the oneness of all life and thought the world itself was going to change radically because of that. As the years went by, I found that not so many people's lives were changed so profoundly as my own. Most people had reverted to the financial and economic pressures of everyday life.

Woodstock was a spiritual event of almost biblical proportions. Although the music was the billed attraction, the main thing was the way the vast majority of people acted toward one another. There seemed to be an infectious quality of bliss. It seemed like humanity was suspended in a different dimension for a while. Many people remember that, and although the media, when it was happening, tried to portray it as a catastrophe, everybody who was there laughed because it was just a giant party, and I don't mean a raucous party, but people found out that spontaneously they could get along well. There was a huge amount of humanity. People were able to interact with each other in a caring way.

Afterward people went to communes, they tried to make changes in their lives and do righteous things. I know some people whose lives are the fruits of those days. They've raised families and they're active in terms of trying to do good things to help change life in their environment and on the planet, and they lead good, wholesome lives. They've explored their inner and spiritual life through meditation and other approaches to realization. So I see many people who were affected. On the other hand, there followed a lot of superficial new-ageism stuff that took on a silly quality compared with the immensity of the transcendental energy at that time.

Aquarius is the symbol of the water bearer, of brotherhood, and that is still real. We are on that cusp, so to speak. We all knew back then that humanity and the planet was sick and that a great purging and purification was going to have to happen if mankind was to live in a more spiritual way. But first the old forces at play were still intact, they had to change, and that wouldn't be easy. So I think to a large degree we're still seeing that. Despite our collective vision of love, peace, and brotherhood back then, we're still living in the middle of a profoundly troubled world. The environmental problems, the way people relate to one another, the wars, the violence. Maybe people are going to have to get sick before they get well. But I think when we talk in terms of the New Age, we're not talking in terms of ten or twenty years, we're talking in terms of a hundred years at a time, just a blink of an eye on the face of eternity. A lot of people wanted it to happen next week.

Woodstock was like a cosmic blast, where we were reminded for a moment. I liken it to the movie *Close Encounters of the Third Kind*, where people were zapped by the light from these spaceships and driven to this place. They have to go, and nothing will stand in their way. In the end, where they're going turns out to be a lovely experience. At Woodstock it was a manifestation of the divine in humanity.

I'm skeptical about trying to re-create the concert. The big challenge is personal and global transformation. The only remedy for changing this planet is profoundly changing ourselves. So, however you get there, that should be, I feel, your pursuit in life.

August 16, 1993

Dear Mr. Landy,

   I am writing this letter to thank you very very very much for the poster and calendar.
   The poster is hanging on the wall in my room. I look at it everyday, thinking how cool it would have been if I could have been there in 1969.
   The calendar is also very very nice. My friends, who, like me, love the 60's, admire the stuff, wishing it was theirs.
   I think if the people of my generation try we will be successful in bringing back the sandals, bellbottoms, tye dye, and the cool music of Bob Dylan, Grateful Dead, and Jimi Hendrix. Then we will be able to bring back the 60's and maybe repeat history by going back up to Woodstock and reliving the past.
   The photos are very nice and it is like being there when I look at them!
   So thank you again. I am very grateful for everything. I hope to meet you one day in the future,either in Woodstock or somewhere else.

Love and peace,

Tracy Campo *(age 13)*

Dear Tracy:

   I was very touched by your letter and excited by the knowledge that there are many young people who, like yourself, intuitively understand and embrace the values of the Woodstock Generation. As much as I would like to be in the sixties again, I realize that we cannot bring back that time, but rather must create a "sixties" of our own, learning from that generation and attempting to improve the future. Woodstock and the sixties were indications of the way we, as humanity, could progress. It was a statement to all the disbelievers, that the world could be one, that with the collective energy formed by loving people, problems could be solved and disharmonies balanced.
   The clothing and music you speak of are very wonderful, certainly they reflect the freedom, positive spirit, and easygoing essence of the time, but life must move on. Today there are many young musicians who are potentially as powerful as those you speak of and they too must be given a chance. Many fabulous musicians have simply not had the opportunity to make their work known.
   Remember also the spiritual books, the metaphysical tomes which inspired the Woodstock Generation. Woodstock was a way of thinking and being, supported by many age-old schools of spiritual thought and practice. Its essence, peace and love, comes from within, and this is what you feel, and why you are so attracted to the time. It's very simple; when you embrace this spirit, you are happy. No matter what travails life brings, you are ready for them, and you use them to grow, to bring you to the next place in your life.
   So look not only to the past, to history, to the archives of record companies, but also to the clubs next door, to the places you can hear music, to yourself, and to the spirit of your own generation, where you may discover your own Bob Dylan or Jimi Hendrix.
   Woodstock was a time of flowering. The festival was the apex of an energy form created by a lot of people who were unhappy with the way things were and who had a joint focus on making a better life. It was an *example* for future generations, not of something to re-create, but of the possibilities that can arise from a time and feeling, including your own.
   Woodstock was an accident that was meant to be. The music was not what it was about. The fashion of the time was not what it was about. *You* were what it was about, you and every other well-meaning person who, although you were not yet born, intuitively understands the values and feelings that were present during the sixties. Love thy neighbor as your brother; trust in the flow of life, that whatever is happening is there to you to learn from; depend on being taken care of by life; share what you have; give what you can. It is for you and all the young people who want to listen that I dedicate this book, in hopes that it may inspire your thoughts and actions throughout your lives, as the things I learned during this time have inspired mine.

Love and peace,

Elliott

Photographs

Henry Diltz, Elliott Landy, Lisa Law, Barry Levine, Dan Garson, Charles Harbutt, Peter Menzel, Shelly Rusten, Joseph Sia, Burk Uzzle, Baron Wolman,

Ralph Ackerman

Cover: Landy
 5: Levine
12, 13: Harbutt
14, 15: Garson
16, 17: Wolman
18, 19: Landy
20, 21: Harbutt
22, 23: Wolman
26, 27, 28: Landy
30 top: Law; bottom: Wolman
31: Wolman
32, 33: Uzzle
36, 37, 38, 39: Menzel
40: Landy
42: Diltz
43: Sia
44, 45: Landy
46, 47: Uzzle
48, 49: Ackerman
50: Law
51 top & bottom left; top & bottom right: Rusten
51 left 2nd & 3rd: Law
52, 53: Wolman
54, 55, 56, 57: Landy
58, 59: Wolman
64, 65: Wolman
66 top: Menzel; bottom: Uzzle
67: Garson
68 left: Garson; right: Wolman
69 top: Wolman; bottom: Garson
70, 71: Sia
72: Diltz
73: Sia
74 top: Sia; bottom: Diltz
75: Wolman
76, 77: Levine
78: Harbutt
79: Diltz
80: Landy
81: Levine
82: Sia

83: Diltz
84, 85: Garson
86, 87: Menzel
88, 89: Uzzle
90 top: Wolman; bottom: Uzzle
91: Wolman
92, 93: Landy
94, 95, 96, 97: Wolman
98 top: Garson; bottom: Wolman
99: Wolman
100, 101: Diltz
104, 105, 106, 107: Landy
108, 109, 110: Sia
111: Landy
112,113: Sia
114: Diltz
115 top: Landy; bottom: Garson
116: Wolman
117: Sia
118, 119: Landy
120: Diltz
121: Landy
121 top & bottom right: Diltz
121 middle: Sia
122: Diltz
123, 124, 125: Sia
126, 127: Landy
128 top: Sia; bottom: Landy
129: Landy
130: Diltz
131: Menzel
134, 135: Wolman
136: Diltz
137: Wolman
138: Diltz
142: Wolman
144: Landy

Ralph Ackerman had been documenting the hippie scene in San Francisco as a photographer and filmmaker. His was the only photography exhibition at Woodstock.

Henry Diltz, one of the two official photographers of the festival, was at the festival site a week before it began. In addition to major publications, his photos have appeared on over 100 album covers, including Crosby, Stills & Nash, the Doors, & the Eagles. He has a dual career as a musician with the band Modern Folk Quartet, and resides in southern California.

Dan Garson, a Connecticut native, attended Woodstock as an enterprising high school student with press credentials that allowed him access to the press box directly in front of the stage. He went on to pursue a career in film, finally residing in Toronto. He succumbed to cancer in 1992.

Charles Harbutt, a Magnum photographer when he photographed Woodstock, brought his wife and children, who left after the first day. He has turned from photojournalism to more personal work, and is presently a partner in the photo agency Actualite.

Elliott Landy, producer of this book, was one of the two official photographers at the festival. Known for his photos of Dylan and The Band, he is currently creating a Woodstock CD-ROM, and working on his vision for interactive music visuals. A book of his other music photography, "Woodstock Vision," has just been published by Continuum.

Lisa Law came to Woodstock with the Hog Farm from New Mexico, where they were living at the time. Eight months' pregnant and with a one-year-old child at her side, she helped to feed 160,000 people while photographing and shooting a film which later became part of her book and her award-winning documentary: *Flashing on the Sixties-A Tribal Document.*She has returned to New Mexico and continues documenting history as she experiences it.

Barry Levine had a camera at Woodstock by chance while working with a sound crew. He has since pursued a career in advertising and political activist video production.

Shelly Rusten's photos of Woodstock have been published and exhibited worldwide.

Peter Menzel went to Woodstock as a college student to participate in the festivities and just happened to bring a camera. He is a California-based freelance photojournalist committed to environmental and social issues. His work has appeared in major publications around the world including National Geographic, Geo, Life, and Stern.

Joseph Sia has been photographing rock and roll stars for the past 25 years. His first assignment was Woodstock, from which he made the book *Woodstock 69*. His work has appeared in numerous other books, magazines, album covers, and exhibitions over the years.

Burk Uzzle, a member of Magnum at the time he covered Woodstock,also brought his family with him. He is a serious photojournalist dedicated to the art of photography.

Baron Wolman, publisher of this book, photographed Woodstock as part of a photo essay he was doing on American Music festivals. He was Rolling Stone's first chief photographer from 1967 through 1970. In 1974 Baron founded Squarebooks,which has published an eclectic list of quality illustrated books and calendars.